INVENTORS & INVENTIONS

NUCLEAR ENERGY

INVENTORS & INVENTIONS

NUCLEAR ENERGY

GINI HOLLAND

BENCHMARK BOOKS

MARSHALL CAVENDISH
NEW YORK

Benchmark Books
Marshall Cavendish Corporation
99 White Plains Road
Tarrytown, New York 10591-9001

Series created by The Creative Publishing Company

Library of Congress Cataloging-in-Publication Data

Holland, Gini.
    Nuclear energy / Gini Holland.
        p.   cm. -- (Inventors & inventions)
    Includes index.
    Summary: Discusses the history, sources, and uses of nuclear
energy and examines its dangers and its possible future.
    ISBN 0-7614-0047-8 (library binding)
    1. Nuclear energy--Juvenile literature.   [1. Nuclear energy.]
I. Title.   II. Series.
QC778.5.H65   1996
333.792'4--dc20
                                            95-44097
                                             CIP

Printed in Hong Kong

Acknowledgments

Technical Consultant: Teodoro C. Robles, Ph.D.
Illustrations on pages 9 and 37 by Mick Gillah

The publishers would like to thank the following for their permission to reproduce photographs:
Dr. Charles D. Bowman, (56); The Image Bank, (cover); Peter Newark's Military Pictures, (18);
Range/Photoreporters, (45, 58); Science Photo Library Ltd., (12, 20, Roger Ressmeyer, Starlight frontispiece, 43, 53, 59, Peter Menzel 7, Catherine Pouedras 8, Alex Bartel 10, 42, Simon Fraser 11, Prof. Peter Fowler 14, National Library of Medicine 17, Argonne National Laboratory 22, Library of Congress 25, U.S. Dept. of Energy 29, 31, 51, 57, Los Alamos National Laboratory 32, James King-Holmes 35, Mere Words 41, Alexander Tsiaras 44, Lawrence Livermore Laboratory 47); UPI/Bettmann, (16, 21, 24, 26, 28, 33, 48, 49, 54); Dr. J. Ernest Wilkins, Jr., (39).

(Cover) Inside the turbine room of a modern nuclear power plant.

(Frontispiece) The Hanford reactor site in Washington State made plutonium for nuclear weapons from 1944 to 1988.

Contents

— Chapter 1 —
How We Use Nuclear Energy

Deep inside a nuclear reactor's fuel pin, a single neutron escapes from the nucleus of an atom of uranium-235. It zips away too fast to hit the nucleus of most U-235 atoms around it — unless an atom of graphite or water gets in its way. When it smacks into one of these atoms, called moderators, the uranium neutron bounces off and keeps going, but now more slowly. This makes it more likely to run into another uranium-235 atom and hit *its* nucleus.

Pow! It hits and splits the uranium's nucleus, which gives off several other neutrons when *it* breaks apart. These neutrons quickly speed away from the split atom. Some are soaked up by control rods. But one neutron from each atom in a fuel pellet hits a moderator, bounces off, and then strikes another uranium-235 atom to split another nucleus, starting the whole process over again. This is called a chain reaction, and when it is controlled in a nuclear reactor, it gives off a burst of energy in the form of heat each time an atom in the fuel pellet of uranium-235 is split. This heat is converted into electricity. The energy of the atom has been harnessed for our daily use.

When Do We Use Nuclear Energy?

When we turn on a reading light or make toast, we don't usually think about the nuclear energy that makes some of our electricity possible. It's hard to imagine that an atom of uranium was split so that we could listen to our radios or wash and dry our clothes. Yet about one-fifth of the electricity produced in the United States comes from nuclear power plants. In over one hundred facilities across the country, trained professionals carefully control atomic reactions in order to produce heat.

From that point on, nuclear energy works the same way coal- or oil-burning systems work to make electricity. Whether the power plant's heat comes from nuclear energy or from burning fossil fuels (such as coal or oil), the heat produced is used to change water into steam, and the steam then turns propellerlike turbine blades. The blades spin a generator, which produces electricity. When the electricity flows through wires from the plant to your home, you can turn on the television or use any other electrical appliance you wish. Without that electricity, our lives would be so different it would feel like camping in the wilderness.

The Diablo Canyon nuclear power plant in California. States that use nuclear power the most tend to be in the East such as Vermont, which gets 78.9 percent of its energy from nuclear power. Midwestern states get about half of their energy from nuclear power, and southern states around 30 percent of theirs.

Where Does Nuclear Energy Come From?

A one-half-inch (one centimeter) long pellet of uranium, which weighs about one quarter of an ounce (seven grams) and is just slightly fatter than a number two pencil, can produce as much energy as 1,780 pounds (801 kilograms) of coal, 149 gallons (565 liters) of oil, or 157 gallons (595 liters) of regular gas. How can something so small give us so much energy? The secret is in the basic building block of all matter — the atom.

Atoms make up everything in the universe, including every cell in your body, every brick in your school, or drop of water dripping from your kitchen faucet. But what makes up the atom? There are three main particles in the atom: protons and neutrons at its center, which is called the nucleus, and electrons that orbit that nucleus much the same way planets orbit our Sun. Just as gravity keeps Earth and the other planets around our Sun from flying off into space, nuclear energy holds the protons and neutrons together in the nucleus of the atom and keeps the electrons orbiting around that nucleus.

If an atom is hit with a force stronger than its own nuclear energy, it can be split apart, or made to fission. When fission happens, the energy that held the atom's nucleus together is released as the atom breaks into two or more smaller atoms. The energy released is called nuclear power.

Fuel is placed in the core of a nuclear reactor. The core is the dark circular area below water. When it is fully charged, the core is sealed with a dome. This dome also contains the machinery used to move the control rods that regulate the temperature inside the core.

The Power Plant Atom

Most nuclear power plants use just one kind of uranium atom to make electrical energy: uranium-235. Uranium-235 is a big atom. It has 92 protons and 143 neutrons in its nucleus (which add together, making its atomic number 235) and is the heaviest natural element. When the large uranium-235 atom is hit by a neutron from outside itself, its nucleus splits. Then, the uranium-235 atom divides into two smaller atoms, called fission fragments, releases several free neutrons, and also gives off nuclear energy in the form of heat.

By itself, that heat would be like a match that burns alone. The match could burn down a forest, but unless it touches some tinder, it quickly burns out. However, when a uranium-235 atom is split into two smaller atoms, some neutrons are freed to become atom-splitters themselves. They strike other uranium-235 atoms in the uranium pellet and free more neutrons, which in turn hit more atoms, creating a chain reaction that goes on as long as there are uranium-235 atoms left in the pellet. It is this chain reaction that makes a sustained nuclear reaction possible: It creates an ongoing release of energy from one atom to the next and therefore gives us a continuous source of energy.

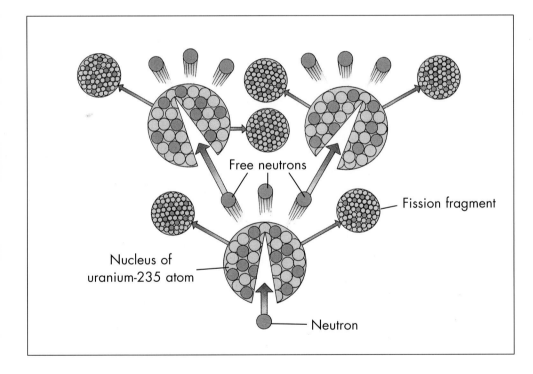

Free neutrons

Fission fragment

Nucleus of
uranium-235 atom

Neutron

This picture shows a nuclear chain reaction. The nucleus of a uranium-235 atom splits into two smaller fragments when bombarded with neutrons from another source. At the same time, the nucleus releases more neutrons, which then bombard other nuclei.

The Price of Nuclear Energy

Coal and nuclear energy are used more than other energy sources because, at the present time, they are cheaper. Nuclear energy is second only to coal as an energy source in the United States, producing enough energy to run sixty million homes. As of 1995, there were 109 nuclear reactors in thirty-two states in the U.S.

Nuclear energy is only one alternative to fossil fuels. The four thousand wind turbines at Altamont Pass, California, provide about 20 percent of the electricity that a conventional power station can produce. In 1978, the federal government started to allow states to make power companies use some renewable, nonpolluting sources of fuel, such as wind and solar energy. However, in the nineties, the government weakened that federal law.

It's more expensive to build a nuclear power plant than to build a plant that uses fossil fuels such as coal or oil. But once the plant is built, the cost of uranium is much cheaper than fossil fuels, and very little is needed to run an entire nuclear plant. This makes it competitive with fossil fuels now. With all our modern energy demands, people are using up the Earth's fossil fuels very quickly, and the scarcer they become, the more expensive fossil fuels will be in the future.

Uranium-235, on the other hand, is relatively abundant and not much needed for anything except energy production. Moreover, a little nuclear fuel goes a long way: A single pound of uranium can produce as much electricity as 480,000 pounds (216,000 kilograms) of coal and only has to be delivered to the plant once or twice a year, which saves on transportation costs. More than half of the people in the world still use wood as their main fuel, but a single uranium pellet gives as much energy in a nuclear reactor as two and one-half tons (two metric tons) of wood! Nuclear power is economical to produce now and will probably be cheaper than other fuel sources in the near future.

What is not cheap is the cost of storing nuclear waste, including everything contaminated by radioactivity when using nuclear fuel — from radioactive mine tailings left when uranium is dug out of the earth to the clothing workers wear in the nuclear power plant, and the spent fuel rods themselves. The costs of possible increases in human health problems and radioactive contamination of the environment could also make nuclear energy expensive — and may be more than the public is willing to pay.

Other Uses of Nuclear Energy

In addition to generating electricity in power plants, nuclear energy is used to power things that must work for a long time before refueling and need a relatively light, small fuel source. For example, some people's surgically inserted heart pacemakers, which regulate a person's heartbeat, are powered by plutonium-238. This only has to be replaced about once every ten years; a big improvement over batteries. Some submarines and satellites use nuclear energy for fuel, which allows them to travel in places where refueling stations don't exist.

Compared to the other fuel sources people have used over the centuries, nuclear power seems in some ways almost magical: It produces no air pollution. Smaller than an acorn that can grow to be an oak, a uranium pellet makes as much energy as a forest of oak trees would provide.

Geothermal energy, another alternative, renewable energy source, uses hot water from deep in the Earth to make electricity. It costs users about the same as wind power. Nesjavellir power station in Iceland makes use of four wells to provide Iceland's capital, Reykjavik, with hot water for heating homes and businesses.

— Chapter 2 —
The Atom and
Its Secrets

Back at the start of 1896, when German physicist Wilhelm Konrad Roentgen first showed people x-ray pictures of their insides — taken right through their clothing — an invisible world suddenly appeared before their eyes. Roentgen named his

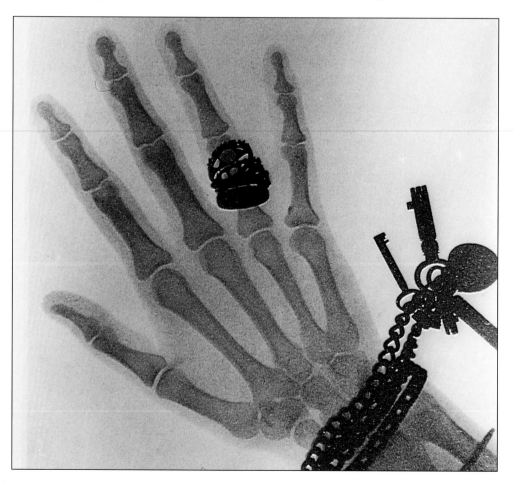

This 1896 photograph shows how penetrating x-rays are. They are able to go through flesh, walls, wood, and clothing but not through more dense material such as bones or metal.

discovery of these penetrating rays "x-rays" because he had no idea what the rays actually were: *x* stood for *unknown*.

In fact, x-rays are electromagnetic radiation waves that have a much shorter wavelength than visible light — so short that the human eye can't see them. They have always existed, but scientists had to use special vacuum tubes to make them occur on demand. Through studying these and other very short waves or rays, scientists began to understand the atom and the power it holds in its nucleus.

Finding the Atom's Inner Structure

In 1897, the year after Roentgen announced his discovery of the x-ray, English physicist J. J. Thomson used a vacuum tube to explore how the electron, a part of the nucleus of the atom, behaves. He noticed that when he sent electricity through the vacuum tube, it emitted a green glow. When he put an object inside the tube, a sharp shadow of the object appeared. He didn't think this shadow could be caused by light waves because light would scatter in all directions and just make a fuzzy shadow. When he held a bar magnet at the bottom of the tube, the "rays" bent down toward the magnet. So they couldn't be light because light cannot be bent by a magnet. Thomson decided these were not rays at all but a stream of particles, each carrying an electrical charge.

Thomson did more experiments to find that these particles were negatively charged and then realized that these particles (electrons) were part of all atoms. He also thought that atoms must also have some positive electrically charged particles to balance the negative electrons and hold them in place.

Thomson thought that the positively charged particles would be scattered around inside the atom. However, his student Ernest Rutherford worked with the big, unstable atoms of thorium. Rutherford's studies gave him the idea of a nucleus around which electrons traveled. By 1911, he accurately

AMAZING FACTS

Both x-rays and radioactivity from uranium are forms of radiation. X-rays are waves of energy, while uranium gives off not waves but actual particles of matter from its atomic nucleus, including protons, neutrons, and electrons. Radioactivity is caused by the decay of an element such as uranium, which loses particles from its nucleus as it ages, while x-rays are mechanically drawn from electrons when they pass near the charged nuclei of anode material in a cathode-ray tube.

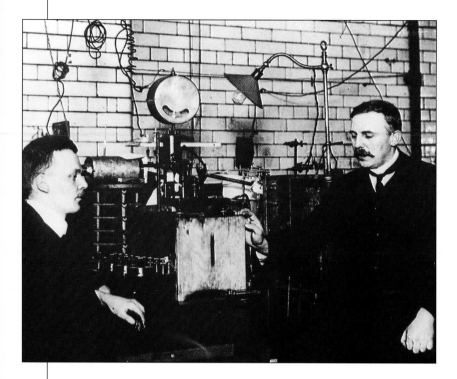

Ernest Rutherford (right) with Hans Geiger in their laboratory at Manchester University, England, in about 1908. Rutherford's experiments explained the structure of the atom. Geiger invented the Geiger counter, a device for measuring the intensity of radiation.

described the atom as mostly empty space, with a central, positively charged nucleus of protons surrounded by orbiting electrons. We now know that some atoms, such as helium and lithium, have neutrons in their nuclei as well. Neutrons don't have any electrical charge, but they give the nucleus of the atom more mass and weight.

The Power of Uranium

As soon as the French physicist Henri Becquerel heard of Roentgen's discovery of x-rays, he got an idea. He knew that fluorescent crystals made of a mix of potassium, uranium, oxygen, and sulfur would glow when struck with ultraviolet light (that part of sunlight that is invisible but makes your skin get sunburned). He thought that these crystals must be giving off x-rays, too. However, when he tested all kinds of fluorescent substances, he found that only those that contained uranium gave off the rays. In fact, even substances that were not fluorescent — but contained uranium — had these rays, and they emitted them whether they were struck with ultraviolet light or not. It was the uranium, not the fluorescence, that gave off powerful rays. Becquerel realized that these were not x-rays and that uranium was a storehouse of a powerful kind of energy no one had really studied before.

Becquerel Inspires Another Scientist

Marie Sklodowska Curie was one of the few scientists who took an interest in Becquerel's unusual rays. At first, x-rays, with their "magical" powers to make people's bones appear on film, seemed much more interesting than rays from uranium.

The first thing Marie Curie wanted to measure about uranium was how strong the rays it emitted were. She knew that uranium changed the air it passed through and made it easier for electricity to pass along the same path. Her husband Pierre Curie and his brother Jacques had made a device that measured even small changes in the flow of electricity through the air, so she could use this to measure how much the air changed when uranium passed through it.

She also tested uranium by exposing it to x-rays, heat, and ultraviolet rays, but the rays remained the same. Then, she tested all the other metals known to her to see if they also gave off rays. Only pitchblende, a mineral ore that contains uranium, did that. In fact, she discovered, pitchblende gave off *stronger* rays than pure uranium did! Why was this? What else could be in pitchblende that was also radioactive, or actively giving off rays?

After much hard work, she and her husband, Pierre, separated the pitchblende into two more elements that gave off rays, or what Marie Curie later called radioactivity. She called the first element she discovered *polonium*, after her native country, Poland. Then, in December 1898, she and her husband distilled a tiny sample of a new element that was close to two million times more radioactive than uranium; they named it *radium*.

But the Curies didn't stop there. They wanted to find out how heavy radium is compared to other elements. Only a very tiny amount of radium is present in pitchblende, but the Curies were quite persistent. They actually processed *eight tons* of pitchblende in order to get the few grams of radium they needed for their work. Brilliant scientists, their biggest asset was their ability to work long and hard to find out as much as possible about the materials they had discovered. Marie and Pierre Curie's persistence made further research on the atom possible and led to the development of both the atomic bomb and the peaceful uses of nuclear power we enjoy today.

AMANZING FACTS

Before the dangers of radioactivity were known, some workers were hired to paint radium pigment onto the numbers of watch dials, so the numbers would glow in the dark. Since these working women used to lick their paint brushes often to make them finely pointed, they took in unsafe amounts of radiation, and many later suffered from bone cancer as a result.

Marie Sklodowska Curie (1867–1934)

Marie Sklodowska had to overcome many obstacles before she was able to pursue the science she loved. Her mother became ill with tuberculosis when Marie was two years old and never hugged or kissed Marie, afraid she would give her the disease. When Marie was eleven, her mother died, which was a financial blow as well as a heartache, because her mother, like Marie's father, was a teacher and provided part of the family income.

Although her family valued education highly, Marie Curie was born at a time when Russia ruled Poland and made it illegal to teach Polish history or language. To make matters worse, girls were not taught Latin and Greek, even though these languages were needed to apply to Russian-run universities. Marie knew she would have to study on her own and eventually leave her country to get a college degree.

She graduated from high school with a gold medal for excellence and for a time afterward secretly went to a "floating university" where subjects were taught in Polish, against Russian law. Then, she worked for eight hours a day as a tutor to earn the money for university studies abroad. After work, she taught at an illegal school for young Polish children for five hours a day and then sent them home so that she could study physics and mathematics late into the night.

When she finally joined her older sister in Paris, she was self-taught in many subjects. She was not very good in French, and it was a struggle for her to understand what her professors were saying. She studied harder, and in 1893, she graduated first in her class with a master's degree in physics. The next year, she returned on a scholarship and earned another master's degree in mathematics. She also met Pierre Curie, a gifted scientist. They were married on July 26, 1895, and began to help each other in their work.

In 1898, Marie and Pierre Curie discovered polonium and radium and, in 1903, shared the Nobel Prize in physics with Henri Becquerel. Generously, the Curies refused to patent or make money from their discoveries. They preferred to give the information freely to the world.

After her husband's death in a street accident, Marie Curie took his place as professor of physics at the Sorbonne in 1906. She was nominated to join the Academy of Sciences, but, because she was a woman, was not voted in. However, the Nobel Prize judges were still happy to honor her and gave her another award, this time in chemistry, in 1911. In fact, she was the first person to win two Nobel Prizes. In World War I, she provided radiology services to hospitals.

In the end, Marie Curie's poorly protected work with radium and other radioactive substances gave her leukemia, a cancer of the blood. She and her husband had even experimented with radium on their own skin, resulting in what they thought were minor burns. She died on July 4, 1934, survived by her daughters Irène and Eve. Irène went on to win a Nobel Prize with her husband, Frédéric Joliot-Curie, for their discovery of artificial radioactivity. Unfortunately, Irène also died of leukemia in 1956, most likely caused by exposure to radiation.

Caricatures of Marie and Pierre Curie in their laboratory. They became famous all over the world and were honored in many countries. In 1921, American President Warren G. Harding presented Marie Curie with a key to a lead box that held a gram of radium.

—— Chapter 3 ——
The Bomb Is Born

After the Curies' first work with radioactive materials, many scientists around the world began to study uranium, trying to discover its atomic secrets. In 1932, the English physicist James Chadwick discovered another particle in atoms. He called it a *neutron* because it was electrically neutral, having neither a positive nor negative electrical charge. This fact became important when scientists tried to split the atom to release nuclear energy because the neutron would not be repelled when it came near the electrical charge in an atom's nucleus. This made the neutron a very good "bullet" to aim at an atom's nucleus.

In 1938, Otto Hahn and his partner, Fritz Strassman, used the neutron to split the uranium atom. Hahn and Strassman knew something was happening when they bombarded the nucleus of the atom with slow-speed neutrons. As chemists, they just weren't sure what was happening.

Lise Meitner, a Jewish physicist who had been working with Hahn, had to leave her work to escape from Nazi Germany to Denmark. Hahn sent her the notes of his and Strassman's work, and on January 13, 1939, she and another German refugee, her nephew Otto Frisch, repeated Hahn's experiment. Meitner realized they had achieved

A radioactive mushroom cloud billows up after an atomic weapon is tested at Frenchman's Flat, Nevada, in 1953.

fission, or splitting the nucleus of the atom and that an immense amount of energy was set free in the process. Her theory helped lead to the development of the atomic bomb, which in turn led to the creation of peaceful uses of nuclear energy.

World War II Supports Atomic Research

Like Meitner, many of the key scientists who helped develop the atom bomb or get support for it were also refugees from Nazi Germany or its strong ally, fascist Italy. In addition to conquering the world, Nazi Germany wanted to kill all the Jews in its path. As the war went on, fascist Italy also began to take away the rights of its Jewish citizens. In addition to Frisch, and Albert Einstein, both of whom fled Nazi Germany, Enrico Fermi had to flee Italy with his Jewish wife. These scientists knew that atomic research was going on in Germany. The Nazis also controlled Czechoslovakia, which had the largest source of uranium in Europe. The scientists had strong reasons to fear that the Nazis would invent and use the atomic bomb before the Allies did.

It was in this frightening world climate that a group of scientists asked Albert Einstein to write President Franklin D. Roosevelt about the possible bomb. He wrote in part, "It may be possible to set up a nuclear reaction in uranium. . . . This . . . would also lead to the construction of . . . extremely powerful bombs of a new type." Einstein thought atomic bombs might be too heavy to be carried by planes, which proved untrue. No one knew exactly how the bomb would behave, and no one could predict how dangerous it would be. They would have to test one to find out.

The First Sustained Nuclear Reaction

To beat the Nazis in this deadly race, Roosevelt started the Advisory Committee on Uranium on October 12, 1939, and asked J. Robert Oppenheimer to head the effort, which was renamed the Manhattan Project in 1942.

AMAZING FACTS

By October 1942, the Allies knew that the Nazis also had another material that could make a bomb — a kind of hydrogen, known as heavy water, made in a factory in Nazi-occupied Norway. Fortunately, Norwegians themselves organized the bombing of the plant and, on February 16, 1943, destroyed Germany's chance of using heavy water to make weapons.

Lise Meitner (1878–1968)

Lise Meitner is seen here with Otto Hahn. They worked together in Berlin for nearly thirty years, until Meitner was forced to flee the Nazis.

Although she pursued the quiet study of nuclear physics, Lise Meitner pioneered in a field largely closed to women and had, at times, a dramatic life. Dr. Meitner was one of the first women to earn her doctorate, which she received at the University of Vienna in 1906. She left Austria for Germany in 1908 to study under the Nobel Prize-winning physicist Dr. Max Planck and served as his assistant at the University of Berlin for three years. There she met Dr. Otto Hahn, a chemist who needed her knowledge of physics to help him in his work with radioactivity. Since women at that time were not allowed at the Chemical Institute where he worked, he and Meitner set up their lab in a basement. He worked on the discovery and study of new chemical elements, while Meitner studied their radiation.

At the start of World War I, they were about to find a new element, but Hahn was drafted and Meitner volunteered as an x-ray nurse for the Austrian army. They continued their work whenever possible and, toward the end of the war, announced their discovery of a new element they called *proactinium*.

In 1918, Meitner became head of the Kaiser Wilhelm Institute's physics department, where she studied how one chemical element changes into another when its atomic nucleus is hit with alpha particles, neutrons, and other "atomic bullets." Then, she and Hahn repeated Dr. Enrico Fermi's experiments to prove he had truly made new, heavier elements when he bombarded uranium with neutrons. In 1934, they showed that his experiments worked. However, sometimes they did not get the heavier elements they expected. Sometimes they got lighter elements. Why?

Before they could find an answer, the Nazis came into power. Her parents, Philipp and Hedwig Meitner, had had all eight of their children baptized and raised as Protestants. However, under Hitler, Protestant baptism was no help. Meitner was fired from her teaching position at the University of Berlin because she was Jewish. Then, Hitler took over Austria; her Austrian passport was useless for leaving the country. To escape the Nazis, Meitner pretended to go on a week's vacation to Holland, where friends helped her get past the Nazi border patrol. She then went on to Denmark. Soon, she was asked to work at the Nobel Institute for Physics in Stockholm, Sweden.

Back in Germany, Hahn and his colleague Fritz Strassman continued bombarding uranium and once again got an element much lighter than uranium. This was evidence of nuclear fission, but since they thought that was impossible, they couldn't believe it. Hahn sent Meitner all the notes of his experiments. She realized they had split the atom's nucleus and called the process "nuclear fission." She and her nephew Otto Frisch repeated the experiments and published their findings in February 1939.

Although her conclusion helped Fermi and others develop the atomic bomb, Meitner was against using her research for war, "I myself have not in any way worked on the smashing of the atom with the idea of producing death-dealing weapons. You must not blame us scientists for the use to which war technicians have put our discoveries." She shared the Atomic Energy Commission's Enrico Fermi Award with Dr. Hahn and Dr. Fritz Strassman in 1966 and died two years later.

Lise Meitner is awarded the Otto Hahn Prize for chemistry and physics in Munich, Germany, in 1955. Hahn himself looks on.

This painting depicts the moment when the first self-sustaining nuclear chain reaction occurred at the University of Chicago in 1942. Enrico Fermi had an extra cadmium control rod held by a rope above his uranium pile, just to be safe. Several men stood on hand to cut the rope with an ax so the reaction could be stopped if it got out of control. They were called "safety control rod ax men," or SCRAM. These initials are still used to name the fast shutdown of a nuclear reactor.

Meanwhile, working from the experiments of Lise Meitner and Otto Frisch, Enrico Fermi and a team of scientists created the first self-sustained atomic fission reaction — where the neutrons released from one split atom go on to hit and split other atoms, which split and hit more and so on — on December 2, 1942. They had brought enough uranium together in one spot — in a squash court under a stadium at the University of Chicago — to start a chain reaction. They called this amount a "critical mass," a mass large enough so that neutrons from the uranium atoms were sure to hit other uranium atoms and keep the process going.

This critical mass of uranium was placed within a pile of material that was 30 feet (9.1 meters) by 31 feet (9.4 meters) at the bottom and 21.5 feet (6.5 meters) tall. The scientists controlled the reaction by placing bricks of graphite between the lumps of uranium. To start and stop the reaction, rods of cadmium (which could capture the escaping neutrons in order to stop the fissioning

of the uranium atoms) were placed among the bricks. When the rods were pulled out, the chain reaction began; neutrons from uranium atoms shot out at other atoms, causing them to split and hit more atoms, releasing energy from the atoms' nuclei.

Fermi estimated that a bomb fueled by such a nuclear reaction would be twenty million times more powerful than TNT, the most powerful explosive known at the time. In such a bomb, the atom-splitting would not be controlled with rods. It would be allowed to go wild, until the entire mass of uranium got so hot that it turned to liquid, vaporized, and finally exploded.

The Big Secret

By this time, President Roosevelt had put atomic bomb research under the complete control of General Leslie R. Groves, who was able to call on the nation's military, industrial, and scientific resources to do whatever was needed to invent the bomb. It took work from scientists in Oakridge, Tennessee, the state of Washington, and the University of California at Berkeley to find and process enough uranium-235 and plutonium-239 for the effort. The bombs themselves were designed and made in the desert climate of Los Alamos, New Mexico, under the direction of J. Robert Oppenheimer. Many American and European refugee scientists, including Enrico Fermi himself, worked together to design and test the bombs. The whole effort cost two billion dollars, with one hundred thousand people working to build two uranium processing plants, conduct research, and make the weapons. Yet, until the bomb exploded, it was all kept a secret.

As vice president, Harry Truman knew nothing about the Manhattan Project or the atom bomb until Roosevelt died on April 12, 1945, making Truman president. By this time, the Allies had won the war in Europe, but World War II still dragged on with Japan. More and more people died every day. Truman went to a peace conference in Potsdam, Germany, and joined the Allies' appeal to the Japanese to surrender. Japan refused.

AMAZING FACTS

Before nuclear fission was discovered in 1939 by Otto Hahn, Lise Meitner, and Fritz Strassman, uranium was used in pigments, ceramic glasses, and a kind of yellow-green glass. It was also used to make steel stronger. Now that it is known to be dangerous to life, its use in these ways is restricted.

AMAZING FACTS

People always die when they are exposed to eight hundred or more rads of radiation. Mice and rabbits can take more than twice that amount before they show signs of radiation sickness, but cockroaches have been known to survive one hundred thousand rads. This is why it is said that, in the event of a nuclear holocaust, cockroaches would inherit the earth.

Albert Einstein (1879–1955)

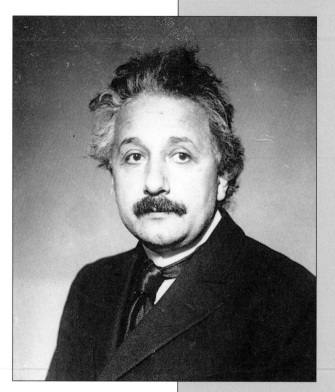

Albert Einstein was a genius who thought so differently from others that he was able to overturn scientific ideas about the entire universe. In 1905, at age twenty-six, he created his special theory of relativity and then developed his general theory of relativity as well as others about how the universe works.

As a child, Albert was considered "slow thinking" and did not talk until age three. From age six and on, Einstein hated school. He refused to answer his teachers, who called him a dunce, while he secretly called them "sergeants." Between the ages of seven and ten, he became convinced that "something deeply hidden had to be behind things." Since he hated school, he taught himself, especially in mathematics. He would often stay up late at night working out geometry proofs.

At seventeen, Einstein was admitted to the Polytechnic Academy in Zurich, Switzerland. A friend took notes for him, so he didn't have to attend the lectures! Here, he met his first wife, Mileva Maric.

Einstein had trouble getting a job after graduation. When he finally landed one as a schoolteacher, he was fired for arguing with the headmaster. Finally, in 1905, he got a job at the Swiss Federal Patent Office.

Einstein's famous equation, $E=mc^2$ (Energy equals mass multiplied by the speed of light multiplied by itself), which he announced in 1906, explains that energy and mass, or matter, are different forms of the same thing, somewhat the way ice and steam are different forms of water. Therefore, when Marie Curie discovered radium, Einstein's equation explained why it was giving off radiation: Radiation is matter that has turned into energy by means of atomic decay. Einstein explained that radioactive atoms lost some of their mass as they emitted radiation. His equation helped scientists understand atomic energy well enough to go on to create nuclear reactors.

On August 14, 1914, World War I began, but Einstein believed in peace. In 1915, he helped smuggle peace pamphlets into countries at war. That year, while a professor in Berlin, he also completed and published his theory of the universe. He then joined Mileva and their two sons in Zurich. But the marriage was not working, and he decided to return to Berlin alone. In 1918, peace was declared, but not between the Einsteins — Mileva sued for divorce. In 1919, Einstein married his first cousin, Elsa.

In 1922, he received the Nobel Prize for "the photoelectric law and his work in the field of theoretical physics." Journalists reported that Einstein didn't read novels or play chess and ignored dress codes but was generally cheerful and playful.

After Hitler came to power in Germany in 1933, Einstein's property was seized because he was Jewish. He fled to the United States, having accepted a post at Princeton's Institute for Advanced Study, which he held until his death in 1955. He was never able to complete his unified field theory, which would explain gravitation (the natural attraction between massive bodies), electromagnetism, and subatomic phenomena in one set of laws.

Einstein with three other members of the World Zionist delegation in 1921. Chaim Weizmann (second from right) became the first president of Israel in 1949. When Weizmann died in 1952, Einstein was offered the presidency but declined.

Atomic Theory Explodes in Reality

Two years after the first atomic bomb was dropped on Hiroshima, this man still had terrible scars. In the few days following the explosion, thousands died of acute radiation sickness because the cells of their bodies had been damaged by gamma rays.

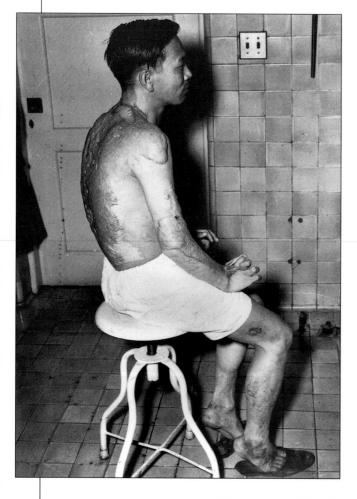

While Truman was still in Potsdam, the Manhattan Project scientists exploded an atomic bomb in the desert of Alamogordo, New Mexico, on July 16, 1945. This was the first above-ground test of the bomb's power. The bomb had the code name "Trinity," but the scientists who had made it called it "the gadget." This bomb was made with plutonium, an artificial radioactive element first made in 1940 by G. T. Seaborg at the University of California at Berkeley.

At that time, scientists did not really understand the terrible power of the "gadget" they had created because they did not understand the life-destroying power of radioactivity. Desperate to get Japan to surrender and end the war, Truman decided to drop the atomic bomb. The crew of the plane *Enola Gay* dropped a bomb, made with uranium, on Hiroshima, Japan, on August 6, 1945. Since the long-term health hazards of radioactivity were still unknown, the Japanese did not fully realize how hard they had been hit and how many innocent people would finally die because of this bomb.

In spite of the horror of people burned alive and severely scorched by radioactivity and in spite of President Truman's warning that the Japanese should surrender or face "a rain of ruin" on their country, Japan refused to give up. Truman then okayed a second bomb drop on the Japanese city of Nagasaki. The bomb, made with plutonium, dropped on August 9, 1945, killed forty thousand people and flattened the city. Five days later, on August 14, 1945, Japan surrendered. The war was over at last, and the atomic age was born.

Chapter 4
A Promising New Power Source

Enrico Fermi's "atomic pile" was the grandparent of all nuclear reactors in use today, including those used for research and those that generate electricity. After he demonstrated on December 2, 1942, that the reaction could be started, controlled, and stopped at will, Fermi and his colleague Leo Szilard drew up plans for a reactor and filed for a patent on their invention in December 1944.

To fully understand nuclear power, scientists still needed to test both peaceful and destructive uses of the atom. The McMahon Bill of 1945 created the Atomic Energy Act of 1946, which set up a U.S. military liaison committee and the U.S. Atomic Energy Commission. This commission was asked by Congress to produce fissionable materials (materials whose atoms could be fissioned, or split) and to manufacture and test nuclear weapons. They were also asked to develop nuclear reactors for military and civilian use and to conduct research in the biological, medical, physical, and engineering fields.

The "Pile" Delivers Electricity

In 1946, Dr. Walter Zinn was named Director of the Argonne National Laboratory, which has facilities both southwest of Chicago, Illinois, and near Idaho Falls, Idaho. Dr. Zinn was not only present for Fermi's first chain reaction: He was in charge of the emergency control rod, called "zip," which he pulled out by

A model of a proposed nuclear power station in Chicago goes on exhibit at an international conference on atomic power in Geneva, Switzerland, in 1955. In the fifties, the promise of a cheap, plentiful energy supply fired people's imaginations and made them think that the atomic age, although it began with two frightening bombs, might lead to positive results after all.

hand to start the reaction and pushed back in to stop it. Under his direction, Argonne became a leading center for reactor development in the country and in the world.

The first reactor project the Atomic Energy Commission approved was for Zinn's proposal to make the first fast breeder reactor, Experimental Breeder Reactor No. 1 (EBR-1), also called "Zinn's Pile." He personally supervised its development at the National Reactor Testing Station in Idaho and brought the reactor to criticality (when enough uranium-235 is available in one spot to start a chain reaction) on August 24, 1951. This reactor generated the world's first electricity produced by nuclear power on December 20, 1951. By the following day, all the electricity in the reactor building was generated by nuclear energy.

Cheap, Clean Power

President Dwight Eisenhower launched the Atoms for Peace program in 1953, hoping to show the world that the United States was dedicated to peaceful use of atomic power. He explained that "the same expertise that built the bombs would be used to develop nuclear reactors." He promised that this would increase the availability of electricity and improve agriculture and medicine, thus raising the standard of living for people around the world. Although he didn't count on some of the big problems still ahead for nuclear energy, Eisenhower was right about his predictions of the improvements it would bring.

Research Leads to Reactors

The Atoms for Peace program helped keep the United States in the forefront of scientific research. By 1954, the country was ready to begin its five-year program to make nuclear reactors. The government gave a great deal of money to private firms and universities to design a working reactor model. Out of the eighty plans they received, the government chose only five for further study and development.

Then, a year earlier than planned, in 1958, the first full-scale nuclear power plant was built in Shippingport, Pennsylvania. It

The Shippingport nuclear plant — the triangular area in the foreground, bounded to the rear by the red reactor building — was built beside the Ohio River in 1958. Three types of reactor were used on the site before it was shut down in 1982. The Nuclear Regulatory Commission now mandates that power companies put aside money in advance to decommission their plants. This currently adds between one-tenth and two-tenths of a cent per kilowatt-hour to the price customers pay for electricity.

was designed to be a pressurized water reactor, able to produce sixty thousand kilowatts of electricity — enough to power seventy-two thousand modern refrigerators. The reactor was based on the original ideas of Alvin Weinberg, Eugene Wigner, and others.

The design concept itself was the work of Dr. Walter Zinn, who also directed the design, construction, and first operation of the boiling water reactor. Dr. Zinn's designs are the foundation of most pressurized water and boiling water reactors in use today.

In the sixties, the Argonne reactor program shifted its focus from water reactors to liquid-metal-cooled fast breeder reactors. This led to Experimental Breeder Reactor II, which had a special, closed fuel cycle. This cycle recovered the plutonium and most of the fissionable uranium from the fuel rods by processes that used remote control and put them back into the reactor so they could be used again. Len Koch, the project manager, and his colleagues, built the facility in Idaho and had the reactor operating by August 7, 1964.

By 1963, one nuclear power plant had begun to operate without government assistance, and by 1966, twenty more plants were producing electricity for private profit. In the sixties and seventies, many new plants were built throughout the country but especially in the Northeast and Midwest.

Nuclear Fuel Brings Hidden Dangers

Nuclear energy gives off radioactivity in all steps of the fuel cycle, from mining uranium to storing spent fuel after it has produced heat in the nuclear power plant. Some forms of radioactivity decay quickly. Decay happens when the nucleus naturally gives off electrons, charged particles, or both. The nucleus thus changes, forming one or more new atoms with different qualities — some radioactive, some not. Many forms of radioactivity, including the kinds used in nuclear reactors, have a very long half-life, the time it takes for half the nuclei in a radioactive material to decay.

This is the biggest problem with using nuclear energy. The uranium-235 used in nuclear reactors has a half-life of ten thousand years; plutonium, recovered when spent reactor fuel is reprocessed, has a twenty-five thousand-year half-life. This means that fifty thousand years from now, in around the year 51,995, one-fourth of the plutonium reprocessed from a nuclear power plant in the 1990s will still be as radioactive as it is today. Since

AMAZING FACTS

Many uses have been found for radioactive materials. Although radioactivity can cause cancer by damaging living cells, when used properly, it can be used to kill cancer cells. As such, it has become a good weapon that helps slow cancer growth. Sometimes it helps patients get rid of the cancer completely. Nuclear technology is also used to help diagnose illness without surgery, sterilize hospital instruments, and to help search for cures for such diseases as diabetes, AIDS, and Alzheimer's disease.

Barrels of radioactive waste are compressed to one-fifth of their original size at Oak Ridge National Laboratory, Tennessee. These barrels contain solid low-level wastes, such as contaminated glass, metal, rags, and equipment. They will be stored in concrete vaults.

the recorded history of humanity only goes back about four thousand years, this amount of time is so far in the future it is almost impossible to imagine what the world would be like at that time.

To imagine that people in the year 51,995 would be able to read warnings we might print on steel containers of radioactive waste is silly: Not only would people not speak or read any of our languages, the containers themselves would have fallen apart long before the radioactive material inside them had decayed. Scientists are looking for better materials to use in storage containers for nuclear waste, but repackaging the waste that is already in containers will be a huge — and expensive — job. Many wonder if society will be able to afford these hidden costs of nuclear energy.

To close a nuclear power plant, it must be turned off carefully to stop all nuclear fission and to dispose of all radioactive parts. This is called *decommissioning*, and it involves removing and disposing of all radioactive components and materials, including some of the water pipes and the reactor itself.

Enrico Fermi (1901–1954)

Hailed as the "father of the atomic bomb" by his fellow scientists, Enrico Fermi was born in Italy as the third child of Ida (De Gattis) and her husband, Alberto Fermi. As a youth, he did poorly in school at first, preferring to follow his own interests. Fermi enjoyed reading at home about science and math and often sat on his hands to keep them warm while he read, turning the pages with his

tongue! He and his more outgoing brother Giulio loved to build electric motors and airplane engines, but his brother died during a routine tonsillectomy in the winter of 1915, and Enrico was left without a brother or a friend. He was sad and withdrawn but began to work harder at school and soon changed from a poor student to top in his class.

At seventeen, he applied for a fellowship and was accepted to the Reale Scuola Normale Superiore in Pisa, which only took students of exceptional ability. In fact, he did so well on his entrance exam that he was questioned to make sure he had not been cheating. He soon became a great practical joker and was almost expelled for exploding a stink bomb in class before he settled down and studied physics so thoroughly that one of his teachers asked Fermi to teach him. Fermi went on to study in Göttingen, Germany, and Leiden, Holland, and taught physics at the universities of Florence and Rome in Italy.

Highly creative, he contributed to quantum statistics and to early theory about beta decay and the neutrino. He was awarded the 1938 Nobel Prize in physics for his experiments with neutrons and used the trip to Sweden, where he accepted the prize, as a way to escape fascist Italy with his wife, Laura, who was in danger from the fascists because she was Jewish.

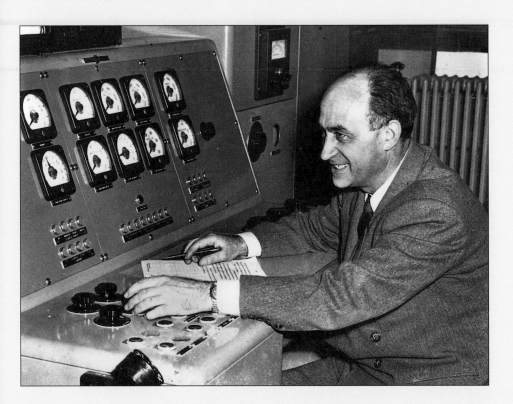

Enrico Fermi at work at the University of Chicago, 1950.

Fermi then went with his family to the United States and, with the help of Leo Szilard (who helped design the "Pile" and gather materials), created the first sustained chain reaction in uranium at the University of Chicago, in 1942. The following year, he moved — with his wife, his daughter Nella, and his son Giulio — to Los Alamos to work on the Manhattan Project. There he helped develop both the atomic and the hydrogen bomb.

He served on the General Advisory Committee of the Atomic Energy Commission (AEC), where he testified on behalf of his friend J. Robert Oppenheimer because Oppenheimer was charged with possibly being a Russian spy. Fermi told the Personnel Security Board of the AEC that Oppenheimer "had rendered outstanding service during the war, that after the war his advice had been given after thorough study and in good faith. . . . These facts offered no grounds for impugning his loyalty." His testimony on behalf of Oppenheimer was cut short, and Oppenheimer lost his security clearance to Fermi's great dismay. That same year, Fermi received the AEC's first special award ($25,000) shortly before he died of stomach cancer on November 29, 1954.

Nuclear Energy Freeze

Safety concerns about nuclear power plants and their radioactive waste have put a stop to new plant construction in most U.S. states since 1978. Many nuclear power plants now in operation are running out of storage space for their radioactive waste, and science, which made such quick advances in putting nuclear energy to work, is struggling to find safe ways to dispose of the spent fuel. Where can we put dangerous "garbage" that takes ten thousand to twenty-five thousand years for half of it to decay?

Albert Einstein explained the challenge of the atomic age when he said, "The significant problems we face cannot be solved at the same level of thinking we were at when we created them." This means we need answers as remarkable as nuclear energy itself. We now have to think in unusually big terms to understand the power of nuclear energy over time. We also have to understand how nuclear energy effects life.

The Fuel Cycle Meets the Life Cycle

When plants and animals absorb radioactivity, it stays stored in their cells. So although radioactivity in a stream of water may be very slight, plants in the stream may be more radioactive than the surrounding water. They have absorbed a little radioactivity every day and stored it in their cells. When fish and animals eat these plants, they take in this radiation and store it in their own cells, where it can build up to dangerous levels. It is the alpha particles, beta particles, and gamma rays emitted by radioactive atoms that enter and damage living cells.

Alpha particles are made up of protons and neutrons and are too weak to penetrate, or go into, human skin. They can be stopped by a sheet of paper. But they are not harmless to living things. If alpha particles are breathed in or come in through food, they can hurt lungs and other body organs and do the kind of damage that leads to cancer.

AMAZING FACTS

Scientists have helped improve agriculture by studying how radiation causes changes in the genes of plants. When radiation makes the seeds of plants change enough, they form new kinds of plants, or mutations. Since some mutations happen naturally from one generation to the next in plants and animals, radiation is just one way that genes can be made to change. Scientists now use this to make new kinds of seeds that resist disease or pests or give bigger crop yields.

Beta particles are electrons. They can go through the skin but are stopped inside the body. They damage and kill cells, as can gamma rays.

Gamma rays are electromagnetic waves that can go right through our bodies and keep on going. In fact, they can go through concrete up to six and one-half feet (two meters) thick. It takes very thick walls to protect living things from gamma rays. If they hit reproductive cells (sperm or egg cells), they can cause birth defects.

Now there are strict laws and guidelines for using all radioactive materials. Special shields are used to protect people who get and give x-rays, and the number of x-rays allowed per year for a person is limited. Animals and people can't breathe radiation out, sweat it out, or get rid of radioactivity in any way once it is in their system except by letting it age or decay. Radioactivity "lives" for many thousands of years, but it can hurt life much more quickly.

Part of a mammoth's tooth is cleaned to make it ready for dating using radiocarbon techniques. Absorbed as carbon dioxide, radioactive carbon is found in all living things. When living things die, the carbon isotopes decay at a constant rate, changing into isotopes of nitrogen. Scientists can compare the amounts of carbon and nitrogen in a specimen to see how old it is.

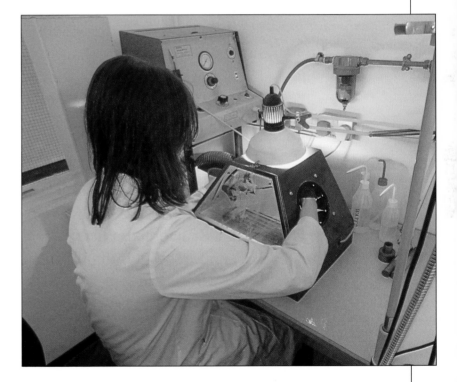

Nuclear energy seems economical in day-to-day operations. However, until a way is found to safely dispose of the radioactive waste, its total cost is hard to measure. If the money needed for safe transportation of nuclear waste and the creation of permanent storage is added to the cost, it may be quite expensive. Health problems related to increased environmental radiation might also raise the price people pay for nuclear energy. For now, nuclear energy is one source of energy we use to meet some of our energy needs, while we try to find ways to harness energy without dangerously polluting our planet.

— Chapter 5 —
Managing the Atom

Many nuclear reactors have been designed since Enrico Fermi produced the first nuclear reaction in December 1942, but all nuclear power plants' reactors are designed to make electricity. Although different in the ways they are cooled or controlled, all nuclear reactors need some kind of nuclear fuel to produce heat. Most (except breeder reactors) use uranium-235. The first neutron in a chain reaction comes from a critical mass of uranium-235, which gives off neutrons as it ages.

Most nuclear reactors surround the fuel rods with a moderator such as carbon (graphite) or water atoms. These slow down neutrons so they will be more likely to hit their targets. Control rods (often cadmium or boron combined with aluminum or steel) are pushed into the reactor core to slow the reaction so that it doesn't get out of hand. They are pulled out to let the reaction speed up.

Reactors also need a coolant to keep the fuel within safe temperatures and bring the heat made by fission to the heat exchanger, which transfers that heat to a container of water. Then, this water boils, creating steam that drives the turbines. A turbine has blades on one end of its shaft, while its other end goes into a generator. The blades spin when struck by steam, and this turns the shaft inside the generator to make electricity. Finally, all nuclear power plants need a safety shield to contain their radiation.

Water Carries the Power in Nuclear Reactors

Two kinds of nuclear power plants in common use in the United States are the pressurized water reactor (PWR) and the boiling water reactor (BWR). The PWR has three water loops separated from one another by pipes, so the water in each loop never touches the water in the other loops while the heat is transferred from one loop to another. In this kind of reactor, water in the first loop flows through the reactor fuel core, where it is heated by nuclear fission. The water in this first loop is kept under pressure so that it doesn't boil, much like the water in a home pressure cooker. When heated, this pressurized water is sent through a pipe that curves through a container, called a steam generator, where it heats the water in the second loop. This water, at a lower pressure than the water in the first loop, boils into steam, which rushes against the turbine's blades to make electricity.

These two reactors both use water as a coolant. The pressurized water reactor is more complex, with three separate water loops. The water flowing through the fuel core is separate from the water that drives the turbine. In the boiling water reactor, one loop performs both of these functions.

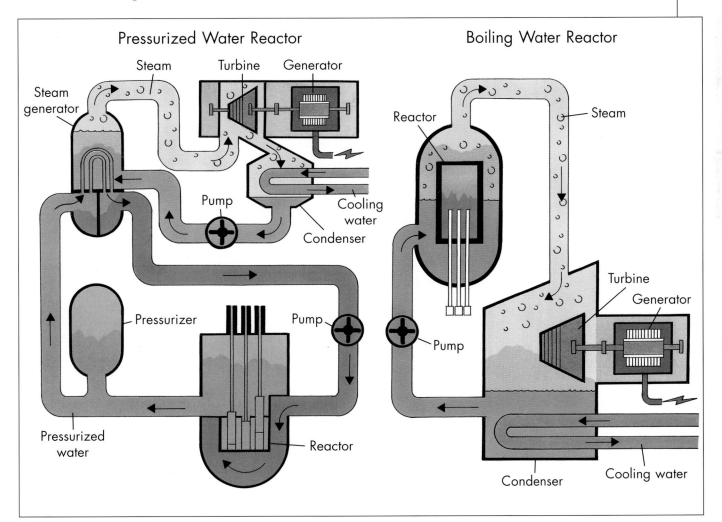

Pressurized Water Reactor

Steam generator — Steam — Turbine — Generator — Pump — Cooling water — Condenser — Pressurizer — Pump — Pressurized water — Reactor

Boiling Water Reactor

Reactor — Steam — Turbine — Generator — Pump — Condenser — Cooling water

J. Ernest Wilkins, Jr.

Can you imagine starting college when you are thirteen years old? J. Ernest Wilkins, Jr., did just that: He was the youngest student ever admitted to the University of Chicago and graduated with a bachelor's degree in 1940 at age seventeen. He then went on and quickly earned his master's degree the following year. By age nineteen, he had earned his Ph.D. at an age when most college students are just completing their freshman year.

Wilkins' parents were also exceptional. His father, Jesse Ernest Wilkins, Sr., was a well-known Chicago lawyer and president of the Cook County Bar Association in 1941–42. In the Eisenhower administration of the 1950s, he was assistant secretary of labor at a time when few African-Americans were working in government. Wilkins' mother, also well educated, was a teacher with a master's degree.

After earning his Ph.D., young Wilkins won a Rosenwald scholarship in 1942 and taught for one academic year (1943–44) at the Tuskegee Institute, one of the first institutions of higher learning for African-Americans. He was then invited to return to the University of Chicago to work on the Manhattan Project in the Metallurgical Laboratory. He studied gamma ray penetration with Herbert Goldstein. Their work was used to help design not only the nuclear reactor but the important radiation shielding that protects living things from the reactor's gamma rays. His work on neutron absorption led to the Wigner-Wilkins approach (named after himself and fellow physicist Eugene Wigner) that allows scientists to estimate how neutron energies are distributed in nuclear reactors. He also wrote papers on nuclear reactor design, operation, and heat transfer.

He then began to work for private industry, beginning at the American Optical Company in Buffalo, New York, in 1946. A superb mathematician, over the span of his career he published about one hundred papers on pure and applied mathematics, nuclear engineering, and optics.

In 1947, Wilkins married Gloria Stewart, with whom he had two children. He returned to the field of nuclear energy in 1950, when he joined the Nuclear Development Corporation of America. He became manager of their physics and mathematics department and then manager of research and development. At the same time, always the scholar, he earned a B.M.E. degree in 1957 and an M.M.E. in 1960, from New York University.

In the sixties, he began to hold offices in the American Nuclear Society, rising to president during 1974–75. He also began alternating between positions in private industry and professorships at universities until 1984, when he became an Argonne Fellow at Argonne National Laboratory in 1984 and 1985.

In 1990, Wilkins became a Distinguished Professor of Applied Mathematics and Mathematical Physics at Clark Atlanta University. He has served on advisory committees for the National Academy of Engineering, the National Research Council, and many other organizations and universities throughout his career, making important contributions to science, industry, and education.

A third loop of cooling water runs through a pipe that coils in and out of the second water loop, where the steam collects after it has pushed the turbine blades. The cool water in the third loop is used to condense the steam into water in the second loop, just the way steam from a hot shower beads up when it hits something cool, like the bathroom ceiling. When it condenses back into water, the second loop's water is pumped back into the steam generator, where it is heated into steam all over again.

The cooling water, brought in from a lake or river, then flows back to its source. It never touched the water in the first or second loop. So the water goes back to the lake or river without directly touching any source of radioactivity. It's reasonably safe; however, it is hot, which can damage life in the water.

The boiling water nuclear reactor only uses two loops. Water in the first loop flows through the reactor fuel core, where heat from nuclear fission boils it into steam. This steam escapes through the steam line and pushes the turbine blades to produce electricity. The next steps are the same as they are in the PWR. The boiling water reactor is simpler than the pressurized water reactor, but it has to be larger to make as much electricity.

More Ways to Cool Nuclear Power Plants

Other kinds of nuclear reactors use something other than water as their coolant. The heavy water reactors (HWRs) use a special kind of water, called deuterium oxide, as both a coolant and as a moderator. The big advantage of HWRs is that they can use unenriched uranium as fuel; enriched uranium is more expensive to make. Unenriched uranium is dissolved from mined ore with acids and then extracted from the acid. This yields a metal that is 99 percent uranium-238 and only 1 per cent uranium-235. To "enrich," or separate, uranium-235 from uranium-238, the ore is converted into uranium oxide and then into a gas that is passed through filters or spun in a centrifuge until it separates. These are a lot of steps to get 1 percent of a metal! So using unenriched uranium is cheaper because it doesn't need all these steps. Unfortunately, heavy water itself is costly, and large amounts of it are needed in heavy water reactors.

In high-temperature gas-cooled reactors (HTGRs), the coolant is usually helium or carbon dioxide, and graphite (carbon) is used as the moderator. Both helium and carbon dioxide allow the reactor core to heat to higher temperatures than water- or heavy water-cooled reactors, so HTGRs can make electricity more efficiently than water reactors and don't depend on a water source.

Organic cooled reactors (OCRs) combine the advantages of HWRs, which can use unenriched uranium for fuel, and HTGRs, which can reach high temperatures. OCRs use an organic liquid (a liquid that must have at least carbon and hydrogen as components) as a coolant, which is cheaper than heavy water, but it is flammable, so the danger of fire or explosion is greater than with other reactors.

A carbon dioxide pump sits at the base of a gas-cooled reactor. Although their fuel consumption is lower, high-temperature gas-cooled reactors cost more to build and to run, overall, than plain water reactors. They are used more in Europe than in the United States at present.

Breeder Reactors Make Their Own Fuel

Although it is often seen as the nuclear power plant of the future, some of the very first electricity produced by a nuclear reactor was made by Walter Zinn's small breeder reactor in Idaho back in 1951. The breeder reactor is amazing in a number of ways. It makes more of its own fuel while it is creating the heat that can be used to make electricity. This is like having a car that makes

The Super Phenix reactor at Creys-Malville, France, is the largest breeder reactor in the world.

AMAZING FACTS

The main kind of breeder reactor is a liquid-metal-cooled breeder reactor, which uses liquid sodium, a liquid metal, as its coolant. Since liquid sodium reacts in a violent explosion if it touches water, it needs a complicated set of heat exchangers to keep the liquid sodium clear of any water contact.

its own gas or a fireplace that makes its own wood. In addition, the breeder reactor does not need a moderator to slow down its free neutrons because it uses plutonium, which does not need slow neutrons to make its nucleus fission. Since it doesn't need a moderator, a breeder reactor power plant can be much smaller than reactors that need moderators wrapped around their fuel elements.

This is how it works: The breeder reactor has a core of plutonium surrounded by rods of uranium-238, the most common kind of uranium. The uranium-238 absorbs free neutrons from the plutonium core and makes an isotope called uranium-239. Uranium-239 is so unstable that it quickly changes into neptunium and gives off an electron. Neptunium is also unstable. It changes into plutonium and gives off an extra electron as well. So now more plutonium has been created. In fact, for every four atoms of plutonium that are used up from the core of the breeder, five new plutonium atoms are made from the uranium-238 rods that surround that core.

Unfortunately, the breeder reactor has technical problems that make it expensive and not as safe as it needs to be. The biggest problem is that it uses fast neutrons, so it's hard to slow down the breeder and harder to control in case of an accident.

Clean Burning, but not Pollution-Free

Compared to other fuels, nuclear power kept its promise to be economical and clean burning. In fact, by 1992, nuclear energy had cut polluting carbon dioxide emissions in the U.S. by twenty billion tons, or 20 percent of what would have been put into the environment without nuclear power. But while it helps cut down on smog, nuclear energy still creates radioactive waste that can harm living things for hundreds of centuries in the future.

Nuclear energy and coal have just about replaced oil as a way to make electricity in the United States. Since most of the country's oil fields are "mature," or getting old, more oil has to be imported from foreign countries, some of which may not be friendly to the United States. They could go to war or refuse to sell their oil at any time. Fortunately, the United States gets energy from many sources, so it doesn't depend on any one source completely. If there is a problem with one kind of energy, the country can turn to the other sources to meet its energy needs.

A French engineer undergoes training on a reactor simulator that duplicates the controls of a real pressurized water reactor. This allows operators to react more quickly and efficiently if real emergencies occur.

Improved Safety

Nuclear power, 20 percent more expensive in the seventies than in the nineties, got cheaper after a nuclear power plant accident on March 28, 1979, at Three Mile Island, Pennsylvania. Because of a combination of human and mechanical error and some serious design flaws, the plant's cooling system failed, so its uranium core overheated and began to melt. Hydrogen gas was produced as well, raising fears of an explosion that would shed radioactivity for miles around. Thousands of people living nearby left the area as the crisis continued for twelve days. The plant shut down after the meltdown was stopped, and new safety standards were written into law so this kind of accident would not happen again.

To meet the new standards, the nuclear power industry decided to put money into equipment and the work force. Improved safety made nuclear power plants more reliable and more productive, which made nuclear energy cheaper to make. During outage time, or time when a nuclear plant is shut down for maintenance and refueling, the plant can't make or sell energy for profit. In 1986, outage time averaged eighty-two days per year, but by 1992, outage averaged only sixty-nine days per year, a large improvement.

Controlling nuclear energy continues to be the biggest concern of the nuclear power industry and the public. Nuclear fuel itself becomes more radioactive when it leaves the plant than when it went in, so nuclear power plants themselves contribute an increased amount of radioactivity on the planet. Many argue that, since this radioactivity builds up in plants and animals and only decays over tens of thousands of years, nuclear power plants are too dangerous. Others hope science and technology will solve these problems and say we depend on nuclear energy too much to stop using it now.

A man wears a special radiation suit and mask to dress and monitor other workers passing in and out of the damaged reactor at Three Mile Island, Pennsylvania. Cleaning up the contamination is expected to take until about the year 2020.

— Chapter 6 —
Nuclear Warnings

When the first atomic bombs exposed people to radiation, scientists had difficulty seeing their effect on health because many cancers caused by radiation only show up twenty or thirty years later. After the atomic bombs hit Japan, doctors tried to help people who had survived but were sick from radiation. They studied the short- and long-term effects radiation had on these victims and found that people do not all respond the same way. The same amount of exposure to radiation can cause enough cell damage to kill one person and not damage other people. However, that same amount may effect those other people's future children. Much depends on where and when the rays strike.

Corbin Harney, spiritual leader of the Western Shoshone people, was one of over 180 antinuclear activists who invaded the Mercury nuclear weapons test site in Nevada in August 1995. They were commemorating the fiftieth anniversary of the bombing of Hiroshima and opposing worldwide nuclear weapons testing. The site, which was used for nuclear testing right up to 1992, is in the ancestral Shoshone heartland.

Safe Levels of Radiation

The basic unit of measure of the biological effect from exposure to radiation is called a *rem*, and safe levels for life are measured in millirems, which are one-thousandth of a rem. Nuclear power plants give off about 0.51 millirems of radioactivity per year — low compared to the average 360 millirems we get yearly from the combined "background" radiation from the Sun, ground, color TV, x-rays, and other sources.

Only at levels of 75,000 to 150,000 millirems do people actually notice any symptoms, such as nausea and vomiting. At that level, most would not have any problems. For those who did, complete recovery would normally occur. Only at levels above 400,000 millirems in a single dose do serious blood complications and some damage to the intestines occur. Single doses above 600,000 require medical treatment and can cause death. At levels of 1,500,000 millirems and beyond, death usually follows, even with medical treatment.

Accidental Warning

No one was prepared for the disaster at Chernobyl. The Soviet reactor had no containment vessel, and its control rods were flammable, made of graphite instead of boron. But it took human error to explode Unit Number Four. N. M. Fomin, the chief engineer, wanted to test whether or not the spinning turbo-generator blades could make up for the loss of power during a blackout. However, he designed his test so that the emergency core-cooling system was also shut down. That was a mistake.

At 1:00 P.M. on April 25, 1986, the power at Unit Number Four was lowered to three thousand thermal megawatts. The turbo-generator continued to generate electricity for the reactor, but it was slowing down; less and less energy was available to trigger an emergency shutdown. Then the emergency core-cooling system was turned off.

AMAZING FACTS

The only dosimeters (instruments that measure a person's radioactive contamination) available at Chernobyl at the time of the accident were not made to measure the large doses of radiation that the explosion gave off, and so the long-term effects on the health of people in nearby towns and on the health of their children and grandchildren are difficult to estimate. At the time of the accident, people had no idea how much radiation they were receiving, and many firefighters exposed themselves to deadly doses in their heroic efforts to put out the blazing reactor. About six hundred and fifty thousand people worked to contain this disaster, and five to ten thousand of those have died so far as a result of radiation poisoning.

The reactor was still fissioning, so it needed at least twenty-eight to thirty control rods in its core to control the nuclear reaction. But the core was filling up with radioactive gases (xenon and iodine-131), and more control rods had to be removed to make room for the gas. The water in the fuel channels began boiling at 1:33:04 A.M. on April 26, causing a power surge. One operator pushed the emergency button to lower 193 control rods into the core, but air inside the hollow tips of the rods expanded in the high temperatures so that the rods jammed. Steam formed, the core temperature soared, and twenty seconds later, the reactor exploded. Radiation showered over the surrounding countryside and nearby towns.

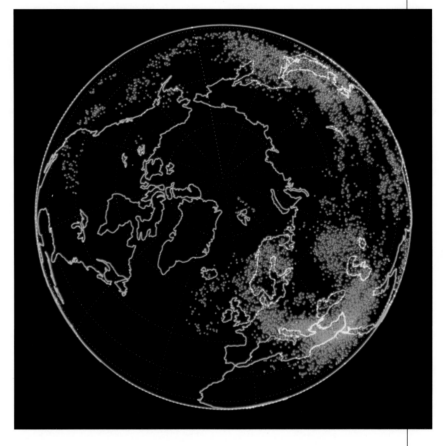

Cleanup was estimated to take over two billion dollars and ten years. The effect this disaster has on the air, food, water supplies and health of Europe and the rest of the world, as the winds continue to spread Chernobyl's nuclear dust, will continue long after the name Chernobyl is forgotten.

What We Know About Nuclear Waste

Even with all safety features in place — and with extra checks to prevent human error — the nuclear power industry contributes its share to the growing amount of radioactive waste piling up on Earth. There are a number of kinds of waste, but they all must be carefully handled.

This computer simulation shows the distribution of radioactivity in the northern hemisphere ten days after the nuclear explosion at Chernobyl. High-altitude winds carried radioactivity over the Middle East and Asia, while low-level winds blew it over Scandinavia. The first world news of the disaster was given from Sweden, where radiation monitors went wild.

J. Robert Oppenheimer (1904–1967)

J. Robert Oppenheimer (left) and Major General Leslie R. Groves view the base of the steel tower on which the first atomic bomb hung at Alamogordo.

As a student, J. Robert Oppenheimer was so used to performing well that he disliked anything he was not good at, including most sports. He wouldn't even climb stairs at school and took the elevator until teachers complained to his parents.

Sparked by his grandfather's gift rock collection, the young Oppenheimer became an expert mineralogist. He became a member of the New York Mineralogical Society at age eleven and presented his first scientific paper there at age twelve. Seen as a "brainy snob" at camp, his peers locked him naked in an icehouse overnight when he was fourteen. A gifted student with few friends, as a teenager he much preferred the company of scientifically-minded adults.

He earned his B.A. from Harvard in 1925 and went to Cambridge to work under the Nobel prize-winner Dr. J. J. Thomson, but he was much better at theory than physical lab work. He hated his imperfect performance and became suicidal and violent, but psychiatric counseling helped. He transferred to Göttingen in the fall of 1926 and received his Ph.D. from the University of Göttingen in 1927.

He then taught at the University of California and California Institute of Technology, alternating semesters, from 1929 until his appointment in 1947 as director of the Institute for Advanced Study at Princeton, New Jersey. At first, he was a terrible lecturer, talking too fast and terrifying his students. Fortunately, he would also tutor them and then whip up a great meal. Slowly, his lecturing improved, and he became one of the best teachers of his generation.

He was appointed to lead a team of 1,550 people at Los Alamos, New Mexico, to develop the atomic bomb. When it was tested on July 16, 1945, he named it "Trinity" and quoted Hindu scriptures, saying "I am become Death, the Destroyer of worlds." He supported international civilian atomic energy control and fought the development of the hydrogen bomb on moral and technical grounds.

Chairman of the general advisory committee of the U.S. Atomic Energy Commission from 1946 to 1952, he was suspended in 1953 — a time of general suspicion and fear of communists — because he had worked in socialist causes before the war. Many scientists thought this unfair, but Oppenheimer blamed himself and his prideful personality. His friends stuck by him, and in October 1954, he was unanimously reelected director of the Institute for Advanced Study.

Ten years after his security clearance was removed, he received the Enrico Fermi Award from President Lyndon B. Johnson. Oppenheimer thanked him, saying, "I think it is just possible, Mr. President, that it has taken some charity and courage for you to make this award today."

Oppenheimer died in 1967 of cancer of the throat. Hundreds of friends, scientists, and government officials came to his memorial service at Princeton and honored and praised him as great scientist, statesman, and teacher.

J. Robert Oppenheimer (left) and other atomic experts look at a photo of the explosion of the atomic bomb dropped on Hiroshima.

The U.S. Nuclear Regulatory Commission divides radioactive waste into high-level waste, transuranic waste, and low-level waste. High-level waste comes from nuclear fuel itself and from reprocessing (the chemical separation of uranium and plutonium from the other elements in the nuclear fuel). Transuranic waste comes from both reprocessing and plutonium used to make nuclear weapons.

Low-level waste includes all other forms of radioactive waste and is further divided into four categories, starting with the least hazardous, A-level, followed by increasingly more hazardous B- and C-level wastes, all of which can be buried in shallow land sites. "Greater than class C waste" is classified as too hazardous to be buried in near-surface facilities.

At present, the United States has no permanent storage facility for any nuclear waste greater than class C. One site, at Yucca Mountain in Nevada, is being studied and prepared for use. Until it is approved, all high-level waste waits in temporary storage, where room and time are running out.

Safety Is Expensive but Voters Insist

In 1976, the Resource Conservation and Recovery Act went into effect. It made all groups that produce nuclear waste get permits from the U.S. Environmental Protection Agency (EPA) and have their activities closely watched for safety. However, safety efforts take time and money, so organizations sometimes try to get around safety laws. Carelessness or cheating at any step in the nuclear fuel cycle can have terrible consequences and must be guarded against.

Since safety measures make energy more expensive, a country that hits hard economic times might have trouble maintaining good safety standards. This must be considered when nuclear waste storage is designed and when planning nuclear power plants for the future.

From the late 1960s on, many voters and elected officials have worked to get tougher laws for managing nuclear waste.

The Hazardous and Solid Waste Amendments of 1984 made the Department of Energy stop releasing radioactive contamination at its nuclear facilities, while the Federal Facilities Compliance Act of 1992 gave the department until 1995 to stop releasing radioactive substances. By 1992, the Department of Energy was decontaminating most of its weapons sites, but cleanup is difficult and expensive, so it goes slowly.

One of the biggest and oldest nuclear weapons facilities is located in Hanford along the Columbia River in southeastern Washington. It made plutonium for nuclear weapons until 1988 but is now so contaminated that its cleanup is predicted to cost upwards of $57 billion over a period of thirty years. The facility contaminated over eleven hundred soil sites, and some of this radioactive waste entered the Columbia River. Here, underground tanks for the storage of high-level liquid waste are being constructed on the site.

International Competition and Cooperation

Since October 1973, when the Organization of Petroleum Exporting Countries (OPEC) began to cut oil shipments to the United States, the U.S. has tried to become more independent of energy imports. In the eighties, as the nation's power needs increased by 50 percent from 1973, forty-six new nuclear power plants were put into service. The country's nuclear power plants were making more electricity by 1991 than all the combined fuel sources had made in 1956.

Nuclear fuel can be reprocessed to make nuclear bombs, so President Jimmy Carter announced a new policy in 1977 that banned reprocessing. Presidents after Carter worked to limit and, with the United Nations, monitor nuclear power plant technology around the world. This has led to problems with countries like North Korea, who say they want nuclear energy for peaceful purposes but may be hiding a nuclear weapons program in tunnels underground.

In 1987, President Ronald Reagan and Soviet leader Mikhail Gorbachev signed the Intermediate-range Nuclear Forces (INF) Treaty — the first agreement to actually reduce rather than just limit the number of nuclear missiles owned by each superpower. With the end of the cold war in 1989, the United States actively began to take apart its own nuclear weapons program and signed a contract with Russia in January 1994 to buy uranium from them to make nuclear fuel, not bombs.

However, in 1995, when Russia wanted to honor an old Soviet deal to sell Iran light-water nuclear power reactors, the United States objected, saying it feared Iran would reprocess the fuel for nuclear weapons. Since the United States controls a big part of the nuclear power industry in the world and makes money from it, the Russian government wondered if the U.S. was just trying to keep Russia out of the sales competition. This and other issues make international agreements about nuclear energy and weapons difficult to work out.

As with Chernobyl, nuclear energy presents safety concerns for the whole world, so international cooperation is important. The International Atomic Energy Agency, or IAEA, was begun in 1957 by the United Nations to make sure nuclear energy is used carefully in all countries. By the midnineties, its nuclear safeguards department had 550 employees and an annual budget of seventy million dollars. This department has recently helped take apart the nuclear programs of Iraq and South Africa with their full cooperation. After the breakup of the USSR in the early nineties, the IAEA also helped parts of that region

AMAZING FACTS

The biggest power of nuclear weapons during the cold war period was their ability to keep the superpowers (the United States and the Union of Soviet Socialist Republics) and others from going to war. Nuclear bombs were seen as unbelievably deadly and destructive to both civilization and life on the planet. This led to a kind of standoff in which no one dared to "push the button" that would start a nuclear firestorm.

protect their nuclear materials, so they couldn't be stolen and used for dangerous purposes.

Safety Concerns

Safety standards are set by the International Commission on Radiological Protection, and these standards are accepted by all countries who have nuclear power plants. In fact, safety measures make up a good part of the cost of nuclear power today. In spite of some serious accidents, the industry has a good record for safety overall.

However, although the Nuclear Regulatory Commission has two people on site at each plant in the United States, daily safety checks are monitored by the electric power companies who own the plants. They might cover up safety problems to keep selling electricity, so many people feel this does not make nuclear power plants truly safe.

Spent nuclear fuel elements are stored under water at the La Hague reprocessing plant, France. Spent fuel rods are left underwater for two years to "cool off" before being reprocessed.

Further expansion of the nuclear energy industry is on hold in most states at present because voters are cautious about adding any more dangers to the environment. Most communities want to wait until solutions catch up to the problems of nuclear waste. They hope solutions will be affordable and ensure true safety now and for future generations.

——— Chapter 7 ———
Energy for the Future

The most immediate need is to find a safe way to dispose of the nuclear waste already created. The U.S. Department of Energy reports that more than twenty thousand metric tons of spent fuel are now stored at more than sixty nuclear power plants, and that by the year 2000, around forty thousand metric tons will have been produced. There will also be about eight thousand metric tons of solid waste from defense programs. The federal government has been advised that the safest place would be to put the waste in a deep underground storage place called a *repository*.

Worries about transportation of radioactive waste through populated areas have already made many communities pass laws against vehicles passing through with radioactive cargo. If and when a permanent storage site can be built, transportation issues will grow as waste is moved to permanent storage.

Scientists will need about ten more years to study the potential repository site of Yucca Mountain, Nevada. Possible changes, such as earth and rock movement and water seepage, could occur over the extremely long period that this repository would have to remain stable. Other sites have already been rejected, leaving only Yucca

Mountain as an option. Even after all the scientific questions are answered, the state of Nevada has the right to veto the plan. That veto could only be overturned by a majority vote in Congress.

The project is expected to cost at least $15 billion. This is quite a price to pay for "cheap" energy. However, disposing of nuclear waste is a problem that must be solved, even if no more waste were ever produced.

Research: An Important Door to the Future

Scientists are working hard to find solutions to the problems of nuclear waste. In 1993, Dr. Charles D. Bowman became project leader for Accelerator-Driven Transmutation Technology at Los Alamos. His team is exploring technology to make nuclear electric power that doesn't create high-level waste as a byproduct. They are also trying to develop ways to put reactor and accelerator technologies together so that nuclear wastes can be destroyed.

Studies so far show that the site of the Yucca Mountain nuclear waste repository is fairly stable, but Dr. Bowman and other federal scientists think the waste itself might start a new fission process underground and erupt in a nuclear explosion. This would shower radioactivity into the air and ground water. This concern was first raised privately in 1994 by Dr. Bowman and Dr. Francesco Venneri, another physicist at the Los Alamos National Laboratory in New Mexico. Thirty scientists studied the possibility, but while they found some problems with the theory, they could not disprove it.

The problem is, the steel containers made to hold the nuclear waste (including some plutonium) will dissolve long before the waste has gone through plutonium's first half-life of 24,360 years and release plutonium into the surrounding rock. The rock could help start a chain reaction the way a moderator does, by slowing down neutrons as they undergo their natural decaying process. These neutrons could move at the right speed to split atoms into a nuclear chain reaction. Yucca Mountain could become a bomb.

Charles D. Bowman

Dr. Charles D. Bowman is such a pioneer in his field of neutron nuclear physics that he has often had to develop the facilities and methods for studying neutrons and atomic nuclei before he could actually study them.

In 1961, Dr. Bowman earned his doctorate in neutron nuclear physics from Duke University. He then continued his research at the Lawrence Livermore National Laboratory in Livermore, California, where he made new accelerator-based facilities in order to pursue basic and applied neutron research. There he and his colleagues were able to use new ways to examine the properties of heavy nuclei, both fissile (able to fission) and nonfissile. This allowed them to find a way to measure how badly nuclear weapons could be damaged by intense neutron fields if attacked.

As chief of the Nuclear Physics Division of the National Bureau of Standards (now NIST) in Washington, D.C., beginning in 1972, Dr. Bowman led the development of new facilities for neutron physics research, so that standards and high accuracy measurements for the nuclear power field and related nuclear technologies could be established. He won the Department of Commerce Silver Medal for his pioneering work in the development of resonance neutron radiography.

Then, in 1982, he was appointed associate division leader for basic research at the Physics Division of the Los Alamos National

Laboratory, where he led the development of the world's most powerful pulsed neutron research facility and, once again, also helped develop the research itself. In 1990, he began, with his colleagues, to develop ways to put established reactor and accelerator technology together in order to both safely destroy nuclear waste and create nuclear electric power that would not produce long-term, high-level waste and also would not run the risk of a Chernobyl-like nuclear accident. In recognition of his work from 1985 to 1992, he was made a Fellow of the Los Alamos National Laboratory.

Dr. Bowman became project leader for Accelerator-Driven Transmutation Technology at Los Alamos in 1993. This technology is being developed to destroy nuclear waste in ways that will give us alternatives to storing radioactive waste in the ground. During the nineties, he became actively involved in studying the proposed Yucca Mountain nuclear waste repository. "We think there's a generic problem with putting fissile materials underground," Dr. Bowman explained. He has proposed some solutions, including ways to treat the waste before burying it, to make it less likely to start a chain reaction if it should get out of the containers into the surrounding rock.

An aerial view of the Yucca Mountain site in Nevada, the location of a proposed high-level nuclear waste repository. Dr. Bowman is researching ways of making nuclear waste disposal safer.

Dr. Bowman and his wife, Nona, have been married since 1956 and have two children. As both a scientist and a father, Dr. Bowman is concerned about the long-term problems of nuclear waste, and he is using his scientific training and creativity to try to improve the way we use nuclear power today and dispose of its waste in the future.

Dr. Bowman's proposed solution is to remove all fissionable material, either through reprocessing or by putting it through his proposed accelerator. Another proposed solution is to make smaller steel containers and place them farther apart, so the neutrons are less likely to bombard neighboring atoms.

Fusion Power

The world of the future could be fueled by cheap nuclear fuel with no radioactive waste. Fusion, the exact opposite of fission, occurs by joining two light nuclei into one heavier one, and clean nuclear energy is given off when they join. We see a fusion reaction in the sky every day when we look at the Sun and every night when we look at the stars: Fusion is what gives the stars their light and power.

One good fuel for fusion combines deuterium with tritium. These are both plentiful: Deuterium can be taken from sea water, and lithium, abundant in the Earth's crust, can give us tritium.

If scientists could get it going, fusion could produce a self-sustaining energy source. However, fusion, or a thermonuclear reaction, starts only at temperatures of many millions of degrees — even hotter than the Sun! Such intense heat destroys anything on Earth that tries to hold it, and a heat source that hot is hard to control. The hydrogen bomb, a fusion reaction designed to explode, needed an atomic fission bomb to get it started. Clearly, that would not be a safe trigger for a fusion power station.

To solve the container problem, scientists in the former Soviet Union designed a clever

A march and candlelight vigil is held in Las Vegas, Nevada, in August 1995 in memory of the victims of the bombing of Hiroshima exactly fifty years before. The anniversary was marked by many other protests across the world.

tubular ring in 1970 made out of magnetic fields. This magnetic doughnut was shaped to trap and hold the nuclei so they could be heated to high temperatures and held together long enough to get a fusion reaction started. The Russians call their design "the Tokomak," but so far it has not been able to create a fusion reaction. Although scientists need to hold the atoms together for at least one full second to achieve fusion, they have not yet been able to keep them together for longer than fifty milliseconds.

Another possibility might be to strike atoms of deuterium and tritium with laser light, which would heat and fuse them together. A fusion power station would need to fire laser beams at fuel pellets about ten times a second to keep a controlled energy reaction going. Designs tested in the laboratory are encouraging but so far, no actual model has been built.

Although the laser technique seems to work in principle, technical problems remain. Until they are solved, we must rely on fossil fuels, nuclear power from fission, and renewable sources — from solar power and wind to geothermal energy. Since we are expected to run out of oil and gas within our lifetime and only have about 190 years' worth of coal left, we need to find good ways to meet our energy needs as soon as possible.

The secrets of the atom can power our world or destroy it, and how we manage this energy may be the biggest challenge humanity has ever had to face.

The interior of Princeton's fusion reactor is checked prior to a test run. The doughnut-shaped design uses a super-hot plasma of deuterium and tritium, confined by large magnets, to attempt to create a nuclear fusion reaction.

Timeline

1896 — Henri Becquerel discovers uranium gives off a special ray.

1897 — J. J. Thomson discovers that negatively charged particles, or electrons, are part of all atoms and that atoms have positive electrically charged particles to hold the negative electron in place.

1898 — Marie and Pierre Curie discover radioactive polonium and radium.

1911 — Ernest Rutherford describes the atom as mostly empty space with a central, positively charged nucleus surrounded by orbiting electrons.

1932 — James Chadwick discovers another particle in atoms that he calls a neutron because it is electrically neutral.

1938 — Otto Hahn and Fritz Strassman use the neutron to achieve fission of the uranium atom.

1942 — Enrico Fermi and a team of scientists working in Chicago produce the first self-sustained atomic fission reaction.

1945 — The United States explodes atomic bombs on Hiroshima and Nagasaki, Japan, ending World War II.

1951 — Dr. Walter Zinn's fast breeder reactor, Experimental Breeder Reactor No. 1 (EBR-1), generates the world's first electricity produced by nuclear power, lighting four light bulbs.

1958 — The United States' first full-scale nuclear power plant goes into service at Shippingport, Pennsylvania.

1965 — First nuclear reactor functions in space.

1979 — Unit 2 of the Three Mile Island nuclear plant near Harrisburg, Pennsylvania, suffers a major accident, but no one is injured.

1980 — Nuclear energy generates more electricity than does oil for the U.S.

1983 — Nuclear energy generates more electricity than does natural gas for the U.S.

1986 — Chernobyl nuclear reactor explodes in the worst nuclear accident in history, killing thousands and spreading contamination throughout Europe and the world.

1993 — The 109 nuclear power plants in the United States make 620 billion kilowatt-hours of net electricity, or one-fifth of the nation's electricity.

Further Reading

Arnold, Guy. *Facts on Nuclear Energy.* New York: Franklin Watts, 1990.

Barnards, Neal. *Nuclear Power: Examining Cause and Effect Relationships.* San Diego, California: Greenhaven Press, 1990.

Chaney, Glenn Alan. *Chernobyl: the Ongoing Story of the World's Deadliest Nuclear Disaster.* New York: Maxwell Macmillan International, 1993.

Fermi, Laura. *The Story of Atomic Energy.* New York: Random House, 1961.

Fradin, Dennis B. *Nuclear Energy.* Chicago: Children's Press, 1987.

Halacy, Dan. *Nuclear Energy.* New York: Franklin Watts, 1984.

Haines, Gail Kay. *The Great Nuclear Power Debate.* New York: Dodd, Mead, 1985.

Hamilton, Sue L. *Chernobyl: Nuclear Power Plant Explosion.* Edina, Minnesota: Abdo & Daughters, 1991.

Jaspersen, James, and Jane Fitz-Randolph. *From Quarks to Quasars: A Tour of the Universe.* New York: Atheneum, 1987.

Kiefer, Irene. *Nuclear Energy at the Crossroads.* New York: Atheneum, 1984.

Lampton, Christopher. *Nuclear Accident.* Brookfield, Connecticut: Millbrook Press, 1992.

Stein, Conrad R. *The Manhattan Project.* Chicago: Children's Press, 1993.

Glossary

Control rods: Material inserted in the core of a nuclear reactor to absorb neutrons and thereby control the nuclear reaction.

Coolant: Any substance that cools fuel to keep it within a safe temperature. In a nuclear reactor, the coolant also brings the heat produced by fission to the heat exchangers that generate steam that drives the turbines.

Fallout: The radioactive matter that "falls out" of, or is emitted by, nuclear material as it decays.

Geologist: One who scientifically studies the origin, structure, and history of the earth's crust and core.

Isotope: An atom having the same atomic number as a regular atom — that is, the same number of protons and electrons — but having more neutrons in its nucleus, giving it slightly different properties.

Kelvin: A unit of absolute temperature, developed by British physicist William Thomson Kelvin, in 1848. On the Kelvin scale, water freezes at 273.15 K and boils at 373.15 K. The unit equals one Celsius degree.

Millirems: One thousandth of a **rem**, which is the basic unit of measure of the biological effect from exposure to radiation.

Moderator: Atoms (such as carbon or water) that get in the way of neutrons, slowing them down so they will be more likely to hit their targets (other atoms' nuclei) and split them.

Rad: The basic unit of absorbed radiation.

Radioisotope: A radioactive isotope, which is a different form of a naturally occurring element, having a slightly different atomic structure. It can be metal, mineral, powder, liquid, or gas, just as elements are.

Reprocessing: Chemically separating uranium and plutonium from the other elements in spent nuclear fuel.

Safety shield: Material placed between radioactive areas and the environment to protect living things from radiation.

Wavelength: The distance between one peak of a wave and the peak of the following wave.

Index

Numbers in *italic* indicate pictures; numbers in **bold** indicate biographies